FEB - - 2019

W9-ATT-474

Petra

by Grace Hansen

Abdo
WORLD WONDERS
Kids

abdopublishing.com

Published by Abdo Kids, a division of ABDO, P.O. Box 398166, Minneapolis, Minnesota 55439.
Copyright © 2018 by Abdo Consulting Group, Inc. International copyrights reserved in all countries.
No part of this book may be reproduced in any form without written permission from the publisher.
Abdo Kids Jumbo™ is a trademark and logo of Abdo Kids.

Printed in the United States of America, North Mankato, Minnesota.

102017

012018

Photo Credits: Granger Collection, iStock, Shutterstock

Production Contributors: Teddy Borth, Jennie Forsberg, Grace Hansen

Design Contributors: Dorothy Toth, Laura Mitchell

Publisher's Cataloging in Publication Data

Names: Hansen, Grace, author.

Title: Petra / by Grace Hansen.

Description: Minneapolis, Minnesota : Abdo Kids, 2018. | Series: World wonders |
      Includes glossary, index and online resource (page 24).

Identifiers: LCCN 2017943150 | ISBN 9781532104435 (lib.bdg.) | ISBN 9781532105555 (ebook) |
      ISBN 9781532106118 (Read-to-me ebook)

Subjects: LCSH: Petra (Extinct city)--Juvenile literature. | Jordan--Petra (Extinct city)--Juvenile literature. |
      Petra (Extinct city)--Buildings, structures, etc--Juvenile literature. | Petra (Extinct city)--History--
      Juvenile literature.

Classification: DDC 939.48--dc23

LC record available at https://lccn.loc.gov/2017943150

Table of Contents

Petra

Petra is in southern Jordan. Historians are not sure exactly when it was built. But they know it was before 312 BCE. That is more than 2,300 years ago!

Jordan

The Nabataeans were desert **traders**. They were also **nomads**. They sold incense and spices, and were very wealthy.

They decided to settle down.

They built a capital called Petra.

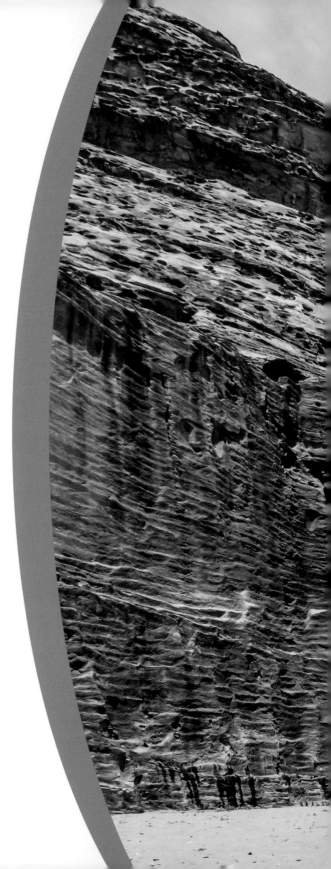

Petra was built between the

Red Sea and the Dead Sea.

It was in a good spot for trade.

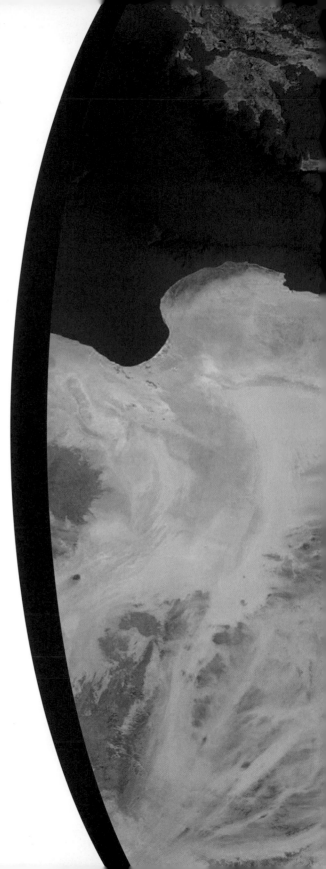

Mediterranean Sea

Dead Sea

Petra

Africa

Red Sea

11

The Nabataeans carved Petra by hand. They then covered it with **stucco**. The stucco was painted with bright colors.

13

The Nabataeans figured out how to gather water. The desert city had beautiful gardens and pools.

15

Historians think up to 20,000 people could have lived there at once.

Roman Rule

Petra **thrived** for hundreds of years. It survived Roman rule and a giant earthquake. People left Petra sometime between 300 and 400 CE. They moved north where **trade** was better.

19

Petra Today

Archaeologists learn more about Petra each day. Only about 15% of the city has been dug up. The rest is still underground. Time will reveal new facts and treasures.

More Facts

- Remains of the Nabataeans's systems of capturing, moving, and storing water can still be seen today.

- Petra has more than 800 structures including temples, tombs, and baths.

- The most important structure is the Al-Khazneh. This is Arabic for "The Treasury." It is a large temple built into a mountain made of sandstone.

Glossary

archaeologist – a person who digs up and then studies objects such as pottery, tools, and buildings.

nomad – a member of a group that has no fixed home and moves from place to place.

stucco – a strong, rough material made of sand and other things, applied while wet to walls.

thrive – to do well.

tomb – a structure built to hold the bodies of one or more dead persons.

trade – the act of buying and selling goods.

trader – a person who buys and sells goods.

23

Index

Abdo Kids ONLINE

FREE! ONLINE MULTIMEDIA RESOURCES

Visit **abdokids.com** and use this code to access crafts, games, videos, and more!

Abdo Kids Code:
WPK4435